G

D0984863

THE STORY OF THE
NEW ORLEANS PELICANS

THE NBA:
A HISTORY
OF HOOPS

THE STORY OF THE
NEW ORLEANS
PELICANS

SHANE FREDERICK

CREATIVE EDUCATION

Published by Creative Education
P.O. Box 227, Mankato, Minnesota 56002
Creative Education is an imprint of The Creative Company
www.thecreativecompany.us

Design and production by Blue Design
Art direction by Rita Marshall
Printed in the United States of America

Photographs by AP Images (Ann Heisenfelt), Corbis
(Steve Lipofsky), Getty Images (Nathaniel S. Butler/NBAE,
James Drake/Sports Illustrated, Garrett W. Ellwood/
NBAE, Chris Graythen, Jim Gund, David Liam Kyle/
Sports Illustrated, Hiroyuki Matsumoto, Layne Murdoch/
NBAE, POOL/AFP, Bob Rosato/Sports Illustrated, STEVE
SCHAEFER/AFP, Gregory Shamus/NBAE, Kent Worner/
NBAE), Newscom (MIKE BROWN/EFE, Ron Jenkins/MCT,
Albert Pena/Icon SMI)

Library of Congress Cataloging-in-Publication Data
Frederick, Shane.
The story of the New Orleans Pelicans / Shane Frederick.
p. cm. — (The NBA: a history of hoops)
Includes index.
Summary: An informative narration of the New Orleans
Pelicans professional basketball team's history from
its 1988 founding as the Charlotte Hornets to today,
spotlighting memorable players and events.
ISBN 978-1-60818-440-8
1. New Orleans Pelicans (Basketball team)—History—
Juvenile literature. I. Title.

GV885.52.N376F74 2014
796.323'640976335—dc23   2013039308

CCSS: RI.5.1, 2, 3, 8; RH.6-8.4, 5, 7

First Edition
9 8 7 6 5 4 3 2 1

Cover: Forward/center Anthony Davis
Page 2: Guard Chris Paul
Pages 4-5: Forward Jamal Mashburn (#24)
Page 6: Center Alonzo Mourning

TABLE OF CONTENTS

COURTSIDE STORIES

INTRODUCING…

HORNETS GO MARCHING IN

THE POPULAR FRENCH QUARTER OF NEW ORLEANS IS THE CITY'S OLDEST NEIGHBORHOOD.

When it comes to celebrations, it's hard to top what happens in the city of New Orleans, Louisiana. Located on the delta of the Mississippi River as it pours into the Gulf of Mexico, New Orleans is known for its annual Mardi Gras festival, which draws thousands of tourists to its famous French Quarter district. "The Big Easy" is also noted for its unique cuisine and, as the birthplace of jazz, for its music. Hardly a day goes by that the city isn't buzzing with energy and excitement.

Adding to this energy is the town's love for professional sports, especially basketball. In the 1970s, New Orleans was the home of a National Basketball Association (NBA) team appropriately named the Jazz. But that team moved to Utah in 1979. More than two decades later, when the NBA needed to revitalize a struggling franchise with a change

of scenery, the league looked to New Orleans. In 2002, a team called the Hornets arrived. Although it eventually changed its name to the Pelicans, it brought with it a 14-season history built to the east, in Charlotte, North Carolina.

The Charlotte Hornets were born at a time when the NBA's popularity was at its zenith. Flush with big stars and abundant fan support in the late 1980s, the league looked to expand into new markets. In 1988, two expansion franchises were added to the league, including one in Charlotte (the Miami Heat was the other team). The NBA enabled the pair of new teams to build their rosters through an expansion draft in

which they were allowed to select unprotected players from existing franchises. After the Heat selected first, the Hornets used the second pick to take young shooting guard Dell Curry from the Cleveland Cavaliers.

Although most of the original Hornets players were either past their prime or inexperienced, as Charlotte's first season unfolded, fans appreciated the play of veteran point guard Tyrone "Muggsy" Bogues, a 5-foot-3 offensive spark plug. They also cheered the team's first acquisition from the college ranks, guard Rex Chapman. "Rex can shoot, he can drive, and he can jump out of the gym," noted Charlotte

IDENTITY CRISIS

When the New Orleans Jazz moved to Utah in 1979, many people thought the team should change its name. Jazz music is an important part of the culture in New Orleans, but not necessarily in Salt Lake City. When the Charlotte Hornets flew to the Bayou In 2002, that team also kept its nickname. But even that had significance to its former city. During the American Revolutionary War, after British general Charles Cornwallis captured Charlotte, the city's citizens wreaked so much havoc upon the English army by firing at soldiers as they went out for supplies that Cornwallis was reported to have said, "There's a rebel behind every bush. It's a veritable nest of hornets." More than 200 years later, the city proudly bestowed the name on its new NBA franchise. In 2013, owner Tom Benson decided his team needed to better represent the city in which it played, and the New Orleans Pelicans, named after a water bird native to the wetlands of the Gulf Coast region, were born. "The pelican is a symbol for our city and region, and we're excited to start a new era in Louisiana basketball history," Benson said.

11

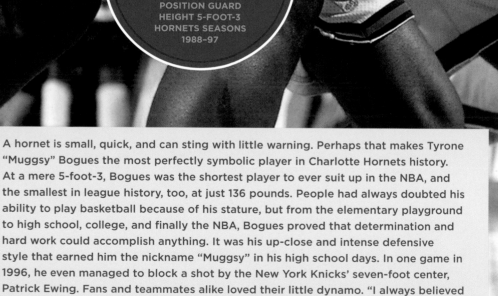

A hornet is small, quick, and can sting with little warning. Perhaps that makes Tyrone "Muggsy" Bogues the most perfectly symbolic player in Charlotte Hornets history. At a mere 5-foot-3, Bogues was the shortest player to ever suit up in the NBA, and the smallest in league history, too, at just 136 pounds. People had always doubted his ability to play basketball because of his stature, but from the elementary playground to high school, college, and finally the NBA, Bogues proved that determination and hard work could accomplish anything. It was his up-close and intense defensive style that earned him the nickname "Muggsy" in his high school days. In one game in 1996, he even managed to block a shot by the New York Knicks' seven-foot center, Patrick Ewing. Fans and teammates alike loved their little dynamo. "I always believed in myself," said Bogues. "That's the type of attitude I always took out on the floor—knowing that I belonged with my talents, my abilities, there's a place for me out there." He proved that little Hornets could sting, too.

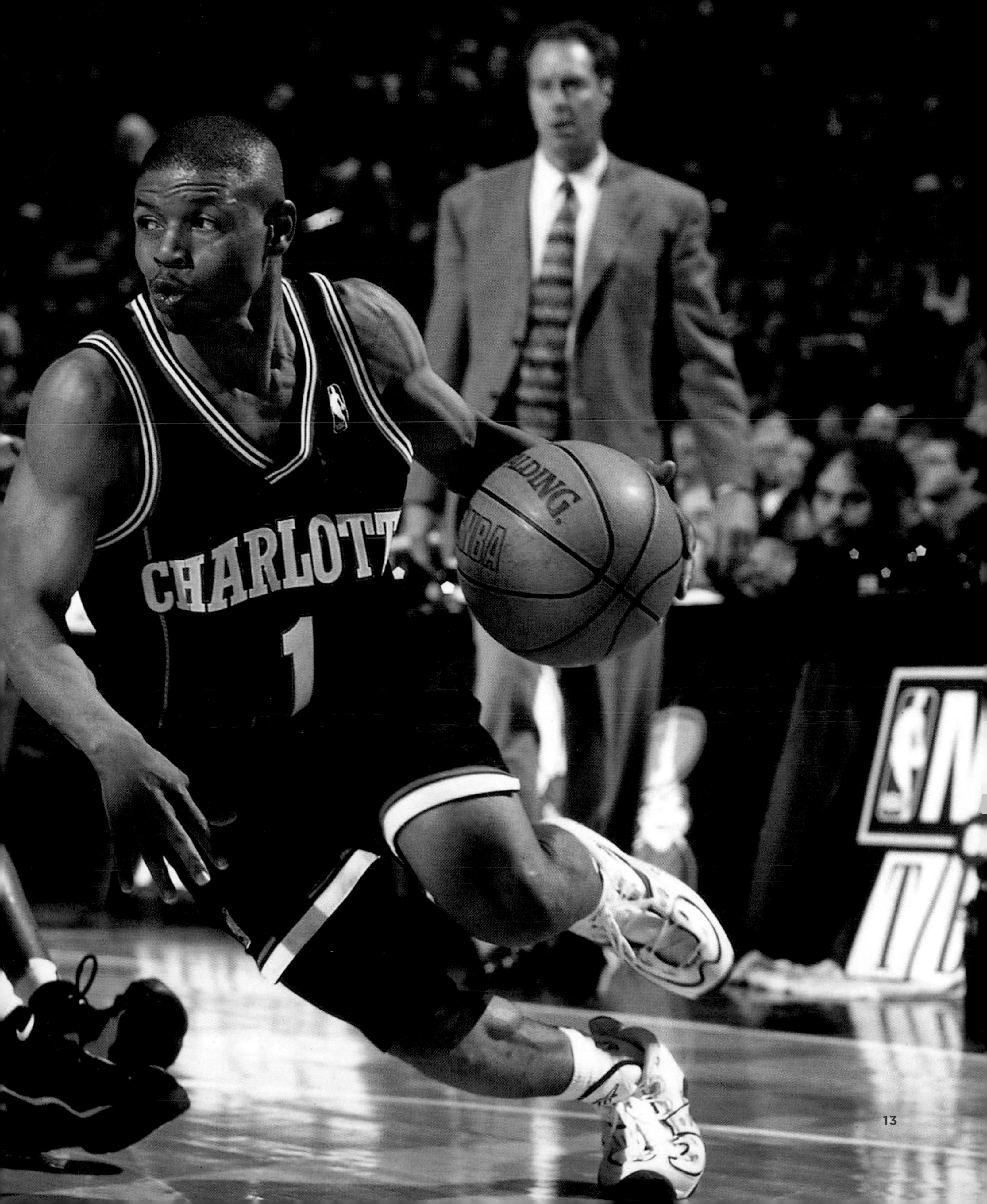
CHARLOTT
1

coach Dick Harter. Unfortunately, the team had few other weapons and finished just 20–62 that first season.

Improvement was slow over the next two seasons. Despite the addition of rookie forward J. R. Reid, the Hornets got off to a miserable 8–32 start in 1989–90. Harter was then replaced by assistant coach Gene Littles, who tried to jumpstart the team by installing a fast-break offense. A new offense did not mean more wins, though, and the club finished 19–63. In the off-season, Charlotte signed swingman Johnny Newman to add veteran leadership to the inexperienced squad. Although Newman averaged a career-best 16.9 points per game, the young Hornets struggled to adjust to Littles's up-tempo style and went 26–56 in 1990–91. Unable to boost Charlotte out of the cellar of the Eastern Conference's Central Division, Littles resigned after the season. Three seasons in, the Hornets needed some heroes.

Under new coach Allan Bristow, the Hornets' luck began to change. In 1991, they drafted brawny 6-foot-6 forward Larry Johnson, who promptly averaged 19.2 points and 11 rebounds per game to earn the NBA Rookie of the Year award. And in 1992, Charlotte drafted Alonzo Mourning, a 6-foot-10 and 260-pound center with strength, agility, and an intense attitude. "Most rookies are a little intimidated coming into this league," said Coach Bristow. "'Zo' never backs down from anybody."

With Johnson and Mourning anchoring the frontcourt, and with Bogues and the sweet-shooting Curry handling the ball, the fifth-year Hornets went 44–38 and made the 1993 playoffs. The young Charlotte team was an underdog in its first-round matchup against the Boston Celtics, but it was brimming with confidence. The Celtics won Game 1 of the series, but Charlotte took the next three to seal the upset, with Mourning hitting the series-clinching shot in Game 4 over star Celtics big men Kevin McHale and Robert Parish. Although Charlotte was eliminated by the New York Knicks in the second round, the Hornets seemed to be on their way.

DELL CURRY

POSITION GUARD
HEIGHT 6-FOOT-4
HORNETS SEASONS
1988–98

He was the very first player the Charlotte Hornets added to their roster when the team got its start through an expansion draft in 1988, and he turned out to be a superb choice. No one has played more games, scored more points, or drained more three-pointers while wearing a Hornets jersey than Dell Curry. During his 10 seasons with the team, Curry was frequently used to spark the team's offense by coming off the bench as the sixth man. A pure shooter, he had one of the quickest releases in the game, making him difficult to stop and the perfect player to provide instant offense when a fellow Hornets guard needed a breather. Teammates knew that if they saw Curry open, all they had to do was get a pass to him, and the ball would be up, away, and likely through the hoop. By averaging 16.3 points per game in a reserve role, he won the NBA's 1994 Sixth Man of the Year award. To this day, the Hornets' very first player is considered to have been one of their best ever.

A STRONGER STING

FORWARD GLEN RICE'S SCORING INTENSITY PROVIDED A BOOST TO THE REBUILT TEAM.

Thrilled by his young team's rise to prominence, Hornets owner George Shinn rewarded Johnson with a 12-year, $84-million contract extension in 1993—at the time the most lucrative deal in league history. Early in the 1993–94 season, however, Johnson suffered a back injury that shelved him for almost half the season. Mourning was sidelined with injuries for several weeks as well. Charlotte had added a new three-point-shooting threat in guard Hersey Hawkins via trade, but without its burly "bigs," the team struggled, losing 16 of 21 games in their absence. Once Johnson and Mourning returned to action, Charlotte made a late-season surge to finish a respectable 41–41, but the Hornets missed the playoffs by one game.

During the off-season, the Hornets acquired the Celtics' aging center, Robert Parish, to serve as a mentor and

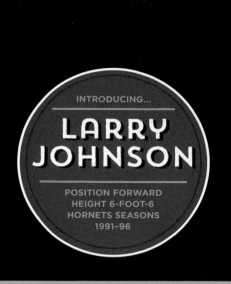

LARRY JOHNSON

POSITION FORWARD
HEIGHT 6-FOOT-6
HORNETS SEASONS
1991–96

Larry Johnson joined the Hornets as the number-one overall pick in the 1991 NBA Draft, and high expectations came with him. Johnson didn't waste any time meeting those expectations, winning Rookie of the Year honors by scoring 19.2 points and ripping down 11 rebounds per game. He was a powerful force under the hoop who would often leave the backboard shaking with his thunderous dunks. The young forward was steady, too, averaging more than 19 points and 9 rebounds per game over the course of his 5 seasons with the Hornets. In 1994, the broad-shouldered, muscular Johnson gained pop-culture fame by dressing up as an elderly lady called "Grandmama" for a series of Converse basketball shoe ads that were immensely popular with hoops fans. While the ads were fun, Johnson's biggest talents were on the court. "He doesn't have any weaknesses," said his coach, Allan Bristow, during Johnson's rookie season. "I've been around a lot of great players in my life ... but all of them had weaknesses. I can't think of a weakness for Larry."

backup for Mourning, who blossomed into a true star in 1994–95. With Zo averaging 21.3 points and 9.9 rebounds per game, the Hornets competed for the Central Division title all season long, coming up just 2 games short as they went a stellar 50–32. In the playoffs, they met the three-time NBA champion Chicago Bulls. The Bulls topped the Hornets three games to one, sending them home with a heartbreaking last-second defeat in Game 4.

After the season, Mourning asked to be paid like the All-Star he had become. Unable to afford another rich contract, the Hornets traded him and two other players to the Heat, getting high-scoring forward Glen Rice, point guard Khalid Reeves, and center Matt Geiger in return. It would be a new-look Hornets team that took the court in 1995–96.

he Mourning-less Hornets struggled after the trade. Johnson was still suffering from his back injury and was no longer the physical defensive force he had once been. Charlotte ended up 41–41 and missed the 1996 playoffs by one game. That triggered more big changes, as Bristow was fired and replaced as coach by former NBA great Dave Cowens, and Johnson was traded to the Knicks for muscular forward Anthony Mason. Charlotte continued to reshuffle its roster in the off-season by acquiring 7-foot-1 Serbian center Vlade Divac in a trade with the Los Angeles Lakers.

Many fans expected the 1996–97 Hornets to struggle as their new lineup jelled, but the team exceeded expectations, thanks in large part to Rice. The veteran sharpshooter averaged 26.8 points a game and proved that he was

still one of the league's deadliest long-range gunners. Charlotte finished with a franchise-best 54–28 record, but the cheers quickly died away as Larry Johnson and the Knicks swept the Hornets in the first round of the playoffs.

The next season, Charlotte traded the extremely popular Bogues to the Golden State Warriors and signed guards David Wesley and Bobby Phills. This new backcourt led the Hornets to a 51–31 record and a first-round win over the Atlanta Hawks in the 1998 playoffs before Chicago brought Charlotte's season to a halt. "We played hard, but we've still got a ways to go to be a champion," said Coach Cowens.

When the Hornets started just 4–11 in 1998–99, Cowens was replaced by assistant coach Paul Silas. Silas had earned a reputation as a fierce competitor during his NBA playing days, and he quickly instilled his own never-say-die attitude in the team. "Paul told us we could sit around and lick our wounds, or we could go out and make something of our season," explained Wesley. The team responded. After making a trade for swift swingman Eddie Jones and lanky center Elden Campbell, Charlotte won 22 of its last 35 games and just missed the postseason.

In the 1999 NBA Draft, the Hornets used the third overall pick to acquire Baron Davis, a point guard from the University of California, Los Angeles (UCLA). With his aggressive, hard-charging style of play added to their arsenal, the Hornets had high hopes as they headed into their 12th campaign. Sadly, early in the season, a car accident claimed the life of Phills and cast a dark shadow over the franchise. The Hornets honored their fallen teammate by fighting to a strong 49–33 finish. But in the playoffs, Charlotte fell to the Philadelphia 76ers in the first round.

MARCUS THORNTON

UNIQUE UNIFORMS

A new team needs to develop its own look, and when the Charlotte Hornets were brought into the NBA in 1988, team owner George Shinn turned to award-winning menswear designer and North Carolina native Alexander Julian for a uniform design. For colors, Julian chose bright teal and purple, and he added pinstripes and pleats in the shorts for a decidedly modern look that was hugely popular with fans. For payment, all Julian asked for was a little "down-home barbecue," which he sorely missed since moving to New York City. Despite the popularity of Julian's original design and colors, the Hornets revamped their look in 2008 to reflect their new home in New Orleans, changing their colors to Creole blue, a darker shade of purple, and Mardi Gras gold. They even put a jazz trumpet with the word "Nola" on the back of the shorts to represent the pronunciation of "New Orleans" in the local dialect. In 2013, when the team changed its name to honor the state bird, the brown pelican, it retained the gold and blue colors but added red and white.

A NEW HIVE IN LOUISIANA

JAMAAL MAGLOIRE EXPLODED FROM THE HARDWOOD TO DENY SCORING OPPORTUNITIES.

The Hornets spent the next year trying to assemble a winning mix of new talent. In the 2000 NBA Draft, they chose rugged forward Jamaal Magloire from the University of Kentucky. After that, they put together a trade that brought forwards P. J. Brown and Jamal Mashburn to town as well. This group meshed well on the floor, playing a defense oriented style that produced a 46–36 record. The Hornets started out hot in the playoffs as they blew past the Heat in a three-game sweep. Charlotte then met a tough Milwaukee Bucks team. In a roller-coaster seven-game series, the Bucks won out, four games to three.

The 2001–02 season turned out to be a memorable one in Charlotte but for the wrong reasons. Mashburn, the player counted on more than any other to lead the team, was injured and missed most of the season. Davis

A HORNETS BUZZER-BEATER

It took the Charlotte Hornets a few years to develop their sting, as the team assembled losing records in each of its first four seasons in the NBA. But during the 1992–93 season, the Hornets were able to score with both power on the inside and sharp shooting from the outside, and they made their first playoff appearance with a 44–38 record. A hard-fought postseason series against the Boston Celtics then followed, concluding with a memorable Game 4 at the Charlotte Coliseum. Entering the fourth quarter, the Hornets had a comfortable 18-point lead. But the Celtics stormed back to take a 103–102 advantage with just 3.3 seconds left in the game, setting the stage for a dramatic finish. Charlotte inbounded the ball to its rookie center, Alonzo Mourning, who dribbled once, squared up, and shot a 20-footer that beat the buzzer to give the Hornets a 1-point victory. Mourning's shot, which triggered a wild on-court celebration, punched the Hornets' ticket to the second round of the playoffs and announced to the NBA that they were ready to compete with the league's best.

> "CHARLOTTE INBOUNDED THE BALL TO ITS ROOKIE CENTER, ALONZO MOURNING, WHO DRIBBLED ONCE, SQUARED UP, AND SHOT A 20-FOOTER THAT BEAT THE BUZZER TO GIVE THE HORNETS A 1-POINT VICTORY."

— ON THE HORNETS' 1993 PLAYOFFS VICTORY

made his first All-Star Game, and second-year forward Lee Nailon stepped up to average 10.8 points per game, but the team still struggled. By spring, it was made public that the Hornets were playing their last season at the Charlotte Coliseum. The team's owners claimed that the Hornets were not making enough money in Charlotte to remain competitive, and they had decided to move the club to New Orleans.

Since the NBA would not grant final approval of the move until May 2002, Charlotte players, coaches, and fans faced an uncertain future. Still, the team was not ready to pack it in. Mashburn returned to the lineup late in the season and posted 21.5 points a game to power the Hornets back to the playoffs. Davis then stepped up to lead the team to a three-games-to-one series win over the Orlando Magic, posting triple-doubles (double-digit totals in points, rebounds, and assists) in Games 3 and 4. But the New Jersey Nets eliminated Charlotte in the second round, and—the relocation having been league-approved by then—the Hornets bid farewell to Carolina and headed some 700 miles southwest to New Orleans.

It was a night of the past versus the present when the New Orleans Hornets opened their season at home against a Utah Jazz team that had once called The Big Easy home. Davis scored 21 points, and Mashburn grabbed 9 rebounds in a 100–75 Hornets victory. The celebration continued as the team then won 10 straight games at the New Orleans Arena. Magloire established himself as a tough rebounder and fierce shot blocker, and Mashburn stayed healthy enough to play in all 82 games for the first time in his NBA career. The Hornets finished their first New Orleans season 47–35 before losing to the 76ers in the first round of the playoffs.

Davis and Magloire were the leading stories of 2003–04, as each put forth All-Star efforts to carry the team back to the postseason. Davis netted 22.9 points and dished out 7.5 assists a night, while Magloire displayed a fiery inside game with 13.6 points and 10.3 boards per game. After New Orleans also brought in veteran point guard Darrell Armstrong to help take some of the load off Davis, the Hornets made the playoffs with a 41–41 mark, meeting the Heat in round one. After dropping the first

INTRODUCING...

DAVID WESLEY

POSITION GUARD
HEIGHT 6 FEET
HORNETS SEASONS
1997–2005

The road to the NBA is far longer for some players than it is for others. After playing college ball at Baylor University, David Wesley went undrafted because, at six feet, he was considered too short to play his natural position of shooting guard and failed to make it onto any NBA roster as an undrafted free agent. Eventually he got a chance in the NBA, but it wasn't until the Charlotte Hornets picked him up that the undersized gunner with the sweet outside stroke found a home. He quickly became a team leader with his tireless work ethic and easygoing personality. Wesley started more games than any other Hornets player and, as of 2014, was second all-time in franchise history in minutes played and three-point field goals made and fourth in total points and assists. "I knew how I got to the NBA," Wesley said. "Fear of not doing my best kept me going. It was always a fight, so I always worked hard." His hard work paid off, as he became only the second player in NBA history (after center Moses Malone) to score more than 11,000 points in the NBA after going undrafted.

two games of the series in Miami, New Orleans won the next two in the friendly confines of the New Orleans Arena. The two teams then traded wins to knot the series at three games apiece, but the Hornets fell short in Game 7 in Miami. "We couldn't get into any kind of rhythm," said Wesley after New Orleans lost 85–77. "We couldn't make any runs."

That bitter defeat seemed to take the wind out of the Hornets' sails. Despite a good 2004–05 season by rookie guard J. R. Smith, New Orleans began to sputter. The team started the year with former Lakers star Byron Scott on the bench as its new head coach, but fans were left stunned by a trade that sent Davis—the team's best player—to the Warriors for guard Speedy Claxton. New point guard Dan Dickau did his best to pick up the slack, but without Davis, the Hornets stumbled to an 18–64 record, the worst in franchise history.

SPEEDY CLAXTON LIVED UP TO HIS NICKNAME BY PULLING OFF QUICK FADEAWAY SHOTS.

A LEADER LOST

In a business in which a game can sometimes seem to be the most important thing in life, reality occasionally comes crashing in. On January 12, 2000, Hornets guard Bobby Phills got into his car after a team practice at the Charlotte Coliseum and drove away. Less than a mile from the arena, he was killed when he collided head-on with another vehicle. Phills's death shocked the team, especially after witnesses reported seeing him racing his Porsche against teammate David Wesley at high speeds just moments before the crash. Phills, after all, was known as a player who was quiet, polite, and never flashy. "The story about Bobby Phills is there are no stories," said Cavs broadcaster Joe Tait. "He was the consummate straight arrow." After a police investigation, Wesley was charged with reckless driving. He joined his teammates in wearing black patches on their jerseys but avoided talking about Phills's death for almost a year afterward. "There hasn't been a day that I haven't thought about him and relived that accident," Wesley said in 2001. "He is always in my heart."

TO OKLAHOMA AND BACK

WITHOUT BARON DAVIS, THE HORNETS STRUGGLED TO EARN A PLACE IN THE POSTSEASON.

The silver lining to that dismal season was that it helped the Hornets secure the fourth overall pick in the 2005 NBA Draft. With it, New Orleans selected Chris Paul, an All-American from Wake Forest University whom many basketball experts expected to become the NBA's next outstanding point guard. "He has great leadership skills," said Allan Bristow, who was now New Orleans's general manager. "We feel he can be a part of an explosive young backcourt for us."

Before the Hornets and their exciting young point guard could tip off their new season, tragedy struck New Orleans. Hurricane Katrina, one of the worst natural disasters in U.S. history, hit the area hard and left most of the city under water. The New Orleans Arena was damaged, and the city's infrastructure was devastated. While the city began to

"PISTOL" REMEMBERED

When the NBA first came to New Orleans in 1974 with the Jazz joining the league as its 18th franchise, the team immediately traded for a local hero, Pete Maravich. The flamboyant "Pistol Pete" went to college at Louisiana State University in the capital city of Baton Rouge. Maravich became college basketball's all-time leading scorer while playing for the Tigers, scoring 3,667 points and averaging 44.2 points per game—and in an era before the three-point line existed! While playing for the Jazz, Maravich wowed crowds with his ball-handling, passing, and shooting skills. He was named First Team All-NBA twice and won one league scoring title. The Jazz eventually moved to Utah, and Maravich died unexpectedly of a heart attack in 1988 when he was just 40 years old. But his impact on New Orleans basketball was never forgotten. In 2002, when the Hornets played their first regular-season game in the city, the franchise retired Maravich's number 7 jersey. "It's a wonderful honor," Maravich's widow, Jackie, said. "I'm really happy to see his number in New Orleans."

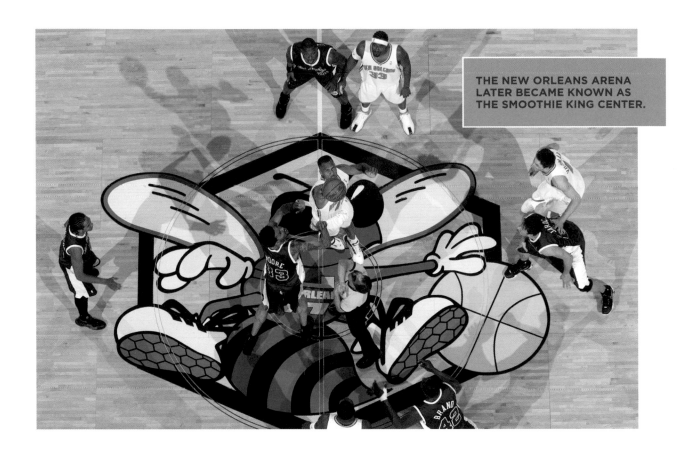

THE NEW ORLEANS ARENA
LATER BECAME KNOWN AS
THE SMOOTHIE KING CENTER.

rebuild, Hornets management signed a deal for the team to play its home games in Oklahoma City, 725 miles away, as the New Orleans/ Oklahoma City Hornets for the 2005–06 season.

In front of a sold-out crowd at the Ford Center in Oklahoma City, the displaced Hornets got off to a fine start by blowing out the Sacramento Kings, 93–67. The team continued to play improved ball after that, staying around the .500 mark. Leading the way was the Hornets' top rookie, who played like an old pro. Paul led all first-year players in points, assists, steals, minutes played, double-doubles, and triple-doubles, earning the NBA Rookie of the

Year award.

Nailon and Dickau were no longer in Hornets uniforms, but playing a supporting role to Paul was third-year forward David West, who blossomed into a star by averaging 17.1 points and 7.4 rebounds per game. West, Paul, and the rest of the Hornets returned to New Orleans to play an emotional game against the Lakers on March 8 in front of a vocal crowd. The Lakers won the game, but the scoreboard was really secondary. It was a giant victory for the fans of New Orleans simply to have their team back home again. Although the Hornets ended up short of a playoff berth at season's end, their

INTRODUCING...

BARON DAVIS

POSITION GUARD
HEIGHT 6-FOOT-3
HORNETS SEASONS
1999–2005

Most point guards in the NBA fall into one of two categories: They're either scoring point guards or floor leaders who run the offense and concentrate on dishing the ball to teammates. Baron Davis not only fit both descriptions while in a Hornets uniform, but he did so at an elite level. Davis took over as Charlotte's starting point guard in 2000–01 and averaged 7.3 assists for the season. That was just the beginning. He soon unleashed a devastating offensive arsenal that featured quick slash moves, a good outside shot, and the ability to dunk on his opponents—qualities that made him much more than just a passing point guard. "When he needs to hit the jumper, he can do that," said his coach, Paul Silas. "When he needs to take it to the hole, he can do that. When he needs to set up other players, he can do that." Although Davis started for only five seasons with the Hornets and missed significant time with injuries, by 2014, he was fourth all-time in New Orleans record books in career assists (950) and fifth in career points (2,728).

CENTER TYSON CHANDLER USED HIS 7-FOOT-1 FRAME TO THROW DOWN HUGE DUNKS.

319

DAVID WEST RECORDED SIX POINTS AND FOUR REBOUNDS IN HIS FIRST ALL-STAR GAME.

38-44 record represented a major resurgence.

The Hornets finished their 2005-06 season back home in New Orleans, but the city had not recovered enough yet to accommodate the team full-time. So, the Hornets announced that they would stay in Oklahoma City for another season, with six games to be played in New Orleans. Beforehand, the Hornets brought in forward Peja Stojakovic to add an outside scoring threat and swung a trade for young center Tyson Chandler.

The acquisition of Chandler proved to be a good move, as he became a force in the paint, averaging a double-double with 11.8 points and 11.7 boards per game. However, Stojakovic was injured for most of the 2006-07 season, and the team was inconsistent, putting together short winning streaks followed by discouraging losing streaks. An ankle injury to Paul cost him more than two months of playing time in the middle of the season and cost the Hornets any chance of making the playoffs. By season's end, the team was 39-43.

The beginning of the 2007-08 season was a happy homecoming for the Hornets. With New Orleans making strides in its recovery from Katrina, the Hornets were able to fly back to their hive at the New Orleans Arena. On the court, with a healthy Stojakovic, Chandler, and West providing multiple threats for opponents to worry about, Paul completed his emergence as a legitimate NBA superstar. The quick floor general averaged 21.1 points a night while leading the league in both assists (11.6) and steals (2.7) per game. Along with West, he earned a spot on the Western Conference All-Star squad as the NBA's All-Star Game came to New Orleans in February 2008.

At the time of the All-Star festivities, the Hornets were the surprise of the NBA, owners of a league-best 37-15 record. A trade then brought in guards Bonzi Wells and Mike James to help the Hornets down the stretch. New Orleans finished the season with a franchise-record 56-26 mark and entered the postseason as the number-two seed in the conference playoffs. The Hornets took care of the Dallas Mavericks in round one and then met another

Texas powerhouse in the San Antonio Spurs in round two. The series played out as a seesawing, seven-game affair, but the Spurs finally defeated the Hornets to move on to the Western Conference finals.

After enjoying the best season in club history in 2007–08, the Hornets put together two campaigns that were largely disappointing. Although New Orleans made the 2009 playoffs, it was quickly drubbed by the Denver Nuggets. Chandler then left town, and Paul missed almost half of the 2009–10 season because of injury. The Hornets had a winning record and made the playoffs again in 2010–11, but huge changes came the following year.

Paul was traded to the Los Angeles Clippers, and the Hornets were back in the NBA lottery. They found some luck there, though, as their name was drawn for the number-one pick. With it, they took University of Kentucky star center Anthony Davis. A shot-blocking sensation known as the "Unibrow," Davis had led the Wildcats to a national championship in his first and only season of college basketball. New Orleans also used a pick from the Paul trade to take Duke University point guard Austin Rivers, the son of then Celtics coach Doc Rivers. New Orleans then signed Orlando Magic reserve

CHRIS PAUL

**POSITION GUARD
HEIGHT 6 FEET
HORNETS SEASONS
2005–11**

The greatest NBA teams have a variety of players. Role players, solid starters, and occasional All-Stars can make any team better. But the difference between a good team and a great team is that the latter usually has at least one superstar. For six seasons, the Hornets had a superstar in Chris Paul. From the moment the point guard stepped onto an NBA court after a brilliant college career at Wake Forest University, Paul was able to hold his own as a solid scorer and one of the best assist men in the league. By his third season, he was the NBA leader in assists and steals and among the elite as a scorer. While his skills made him a star, his leadership made his team a winner. Off the court, Paul was fun and friendly, but when the game was on, he was one of the most intense competitors in the game—an on-court motivator for younger players who wasn't afraid to bark at even his more experienced teammates. When he was traded to the Los Angeles Clippers in 2011, Paul tweeted: "THANK YOU NEW ORLEANS for 6 of the BEST years of my life."

GUARD JRUE HOLIDAY (#11) AVERAGED 7.9 ASSISTS PER GAME IN AN INJURY-SHORTENED 2013–14.

ALL-STAR CITY

In the aftermath of Hurricane Katrina, New Orleans needed to show the world that it was ready to be in the limelight again. The NBA granted the city that opportunity by allowing the New Orleans Arena to host the 2008 All-Star Game. The Hornets had two of their own players on the Western Conference roster as point guard Chris Paul and forward David West made their first All-Star appearances. The weekend featured a spectacular Slam Dunk Contest that Orlando Magic star center Dwight Howard won with a variety of highflying and creative dunks, including his famous "Superman" slam. The Eastern Conference All-Stars won the game 134–128, but the Hornets' 2 All-Stars posted a combined 22 points, and Paul dished out 14 assists. Hosting the event was special for Hornets fans and Louisiana residents alike. "It really shows that the NBA does care about the city of New Orleans," said Hornets coach Byron Scott. "Hopefully when this is all said and done, it shines a spotlight on the city and lets people around the world know that the city is trying to recover."

"WE'LL ALL BE WILLING TO LEARN. WE'RE REBUILDING. WE ALL HAVE CONFIDENCE IN EACH OTHER."

— ANTHONY DAVIS ON THE PELICANS' FUTURE

Ryan Anderson, who was voted the NBA's Most Improved Player the previous season. "We're a young team," Davis admitted. "We'll all be willing to learn. We're rebuilding. We all have confidence in each other. Great coach in Coach (Monty) Williams, great ownership. It's just being ready. I think we'll be fine this year."

ew Orleans missed out on the playoffs again in 2012–13, but fans could see the team getting back on track after a strong rookie season by Davis and some exciting guard play by shooter Eric Gordon and the team's top assist man, Greivis Vasquez. After the season, the team nickname was changed from Hornets to Pelicans, and New Orleans looked as though it would soon be flying once again.

Before the next season, the Pelicans traded for All-Star guard Jrue Holiday and swingman Tyreke Evans, but the changes didn't translate into a winning record. Holiday, Anderson, and seven-foot center Jason Smith all found themselves sidelined with season-ending injuries as New Orleans finished far from playoff contention. Still, Evans stepped up into a starting role, while the rest of the squad played their best basketball late in the season, giving fans hope that the youthful roster would lay the groundwork for a future postseason run.

In two decades of basketball, the Hornets/Pelicans have had to find their way. They've made their home in the "Queen City" of Charlotte, The Big Easy of New Orleans, and even made a stop in the OKC (Oklahoma City) following a devastating hurricane. Along the way, there have been spectacular victories as well as tough losses. But the team has settled into its home, found a new name of Pelicans, and intends to soon compete for an NBA championship and give the city of New Orleans another reason to celebrate.

INDEX